easy BANJO TAB EDITION

JUST FOR FUN

EASY ROCK BANJO

12 GREAT ROCK SONGS—JUST A FEW CHORDS
ARRANGED BY AARON STANG AND ANDREW DUBROCK

Produced by
Alfred Music Publishing Co., Inc.
P.O. Box 10003
Van Nuys, CA 91410-0003
alfred.com

Printed in USA.

ISBN-10: 0-7390-6463-0
ISBN-13: 978-0-7390-6463-4

Cover Photos
Central image models: Katrina Hruschka and Andrew Callahan / Photographer: Brian Immke, www.adeptstudios.com
Mastertone banjo: courtesy of Gibson USA • Moon: courtesy of The Library of Congress • Gramophone: © istockphoto / Faruk Tasdemir
MP3 player: © istockphoto / tpopova • Microphone: © istockphoto / Graffizone • Handstand: © istockphoto / jhorrocks
Jumping woman: © istockphoto / Dan Wilton • Woman and radio: courtesy of The Library of Congress • Sneakers: © istockphoto / ozgurdonmaz
Background: image copyright Elise Gravel, 2009, used under license from Shutterstock.com

 Contents printed on 100% recycled paper.

FOREWORD

Easy Rock Banjo is designed for your total enjoyment. Each featured song is inherently simple, with just a few chords. All the tunes are arranged for banjo from the actual guitar parts, simplified just enough to keep them fun and musically satisfying. Plus, in many cases we've included banjo roll patterns to add to the fun. Make sure to listen to the original recordings so you know how these parts should sound before you start trying to learn them. But most important, just have fun!

—Aaron Stang, Arranger and Editor
Alfred Music Publishing Co., Inc.

CONTENTS

AS TEARS GO BY

Words and Music by
MICK JAGGER, KEITH RICHARDS
and ANDREW LOOG OLDHAM

Moderately ♩ = 112

% Verse:

1. It is the__ eve - ning of the day.__
2. My rich - es__ can't buy ev - 'ry - thing.__
3. It is the__ eve - ning of the day.__
4. *Instrumental*

I sit and__ watch the__ chil - dren play.__
I want to__ hear the__ chil - dren sing.__
I sit and__ watch the__ chil - dren play.__

As Tears Go By - 2 - 1

Smil-ing fac - es__ I can see,__ but not for__
All I hear____ is the sound__ of rain fall - ing__
Do - in' things I__ used to do,__ they think are__

me.__ the ground.
on__ the ground. I sit and watch as tears go by._____
new.__

1.2. 3. D.S. 𝄋 4. D.S. 𝄋 and fade

BIG YELLOW TAXI

Brightly ♩ = 171

Words and Music by
JONI MITCHELL

Intro:

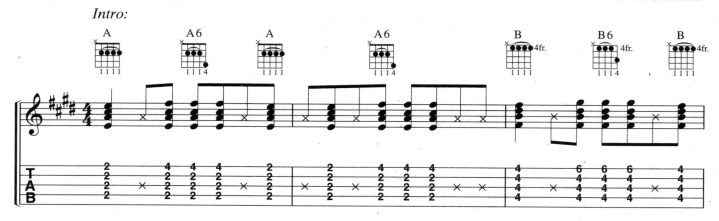

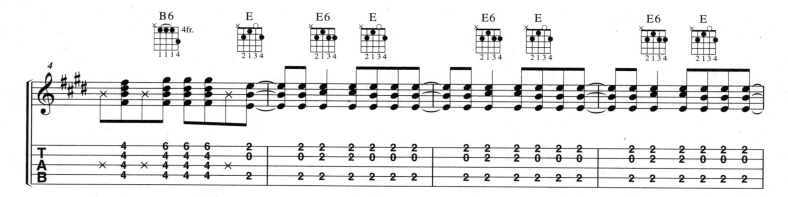

Verse:

1. They paved par - a - dise,_ put up a park - ing lot._
2.3.4. *See additional lyrics*

Cont. in slashes

Opt. fingerpicking pattern

Big Yellow Taxi - 3 - 1

8

Verse 2:
They took all the trees,
Put 'em in a tree museum.
And they charged the people
A dollar and a half just to see 'em.
(To Chorus:)

Verse 3:
Hey farmer, farmer,
Put away that DDT now.
Give me spots on my apples,
But leave me the birds and the bees,
Please!
(To Chorus:)

Verse 4:
Late last night
I heard the screen door slam.
And a big yellow taxi
Took away my old man.
(To Chorus:)

CASEY JONES

Words by
ROBERT HUNTER
Music by
JERRY GARCIA

Driv-ing that train,_ high on co - caine,_ Ca - sey Jones,_ you'd bet - ter watch your speed._

Trou - ble a - head,_ trou - ble be - hind,_ and you know that no - tion

10

Chorus:

Verse 4:
Trouble with you is the trouble with me,
Got two good eyes but you still don't see.
Come 'round the bend, you know it's the end,
The fireman screams and the engine just gleams.
(To Chorus:)

GIMME SOME LOVIN'

Moderately fast ♩ = 147

Intro:

Words and Music by
STEVE WINWOOD, MUFF WINWOOD
and SPENCER DAVIS

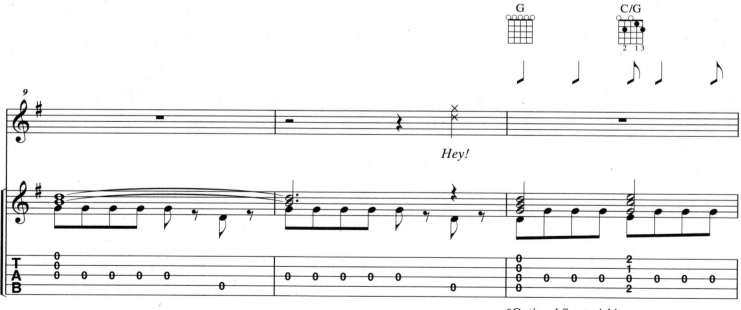

*Optional fingerpicking pattern
(or go to slash rhythm part).*

Gimme Some Lovin' - 4 - 1

14

GLORIA

Moderately ♩ = 124

Intro:

Words and Music by
VAN MORRISON

1. I'd like to tell you 'bout my ba-by, you know, she comes a-round._

2. *See additional lyrics*

Just a-bout five feet four,____

from her head to the ground._ You know,_ she comes a-round here,_

I'm gon - na shout_ it ev - 'ry day.   Yeah, yeah,_

(Glo - ri - a.   Glo - ri - a.)

— yeah, yeah, yeah, yeah.

Verse 2: (Half Spoken)
She comes around here
Just about midnight.
She make me feel so good,
I wanna say she make me feel alright.
Comes walkin' down my street,
Watch her come to my house.
She knocks upon my door,
And then she comes to my room.
Then she makes me feel alright,
G-l-o-r-i-a.
(To Chorus:)

MARGARITAVILLE

Words and Music by
JIMMY BUFFETT

1. Nib - blin' on sponge - cake,
2.*3.4. *See additional lyrics*
*Verse 3 "Lost" verse (Live version only)

watch-in' the sun___ bake; all of those tour - ists cov-ered with oil.___

Strum-min' my six___ string,

on my front porch___ swing. Smell those shrimp;___

Margaritaville - 3 - 1

Lyrics:

Yes, and some_ peo-ple claim_ that there's_ a wom - an to blame_____ and I know_ it's my own_ damn fault.___

Verse 2:
Don't know the reason,
I stayed here all season
With nothing to show but this brand-new tattoo.
But it's a real beauty,
A Mexican cutie,
How it got here I haven't a clue.
(To Chorus:)

*Verse 3:
Old men in tank tops
Cruising the gift shops
Checking out the chiquitas down by the shore.
They dream about weight loss,
Wish they could be their own boss.
Those three-day vacations become such a bore.

*"Lost" verse (Live version only)

Verse 4:
I blew out my flip-flop,
Stepped on a pop-top;
Cut my heel, had to cruise on back home.
But there's booze in the blender,
And soon it will render
That frozen concoction that helps me hang on.
(To Chorus:)

MOONDANCE

Words and Music by
VAN MORRISON

*Optional picking pattern for instrumental section.

TAKE ME HOME, COUNTRY ROADS

Words and Music by
JOHN DENVER, BILL DANOFF
and TAFFY NIVERT

Moderately bright in 2 ♩ = 86

Take Me Home, Country Roads - 3 - 1

28

Chorus:

GOOD RIDDANCE (TIME OF YOUR LIFE)

Lyrics by BILLIE JOE
Music by BILLIE JOE and GREEN DAY

Chorus:

some-thing un - pre - dict - a - ble,___ but some-thing un - - pre-dict-

- a - ble,___ but hope you had___ the time_____ of___ your life.___

It's

some - thing un - pre - dict - a - ble,___ but in the end___ is right.___

___ I hope you had___ the time_____ of___ your life.___

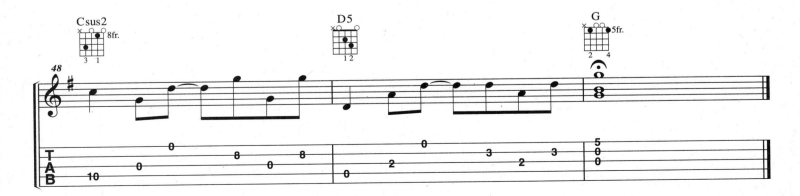

PEACEFUL EASY FEELING

Moderate country rock ♩ = 144

Words and Music by
JACK TEMPCHIN

Verse 2:
And I found out a long time ago
What a woman can do to your soul.
Ah, but she can't take you anyway,
You don't already know how to go.
(To Chorus:)

Verse 3:
Instrumental

Verse 4:
I get this feelin' I may know you
As a lover and a friend.
But this voice keeps whispering in my other ear,
Tells me I may never see you again.
(To Chorus:)

TAKE IT EASY

Words and Music by
JACKSON BROWNE
and GLENN FREY

Moderately ♩ = 138

Intro:

1. Well, I'm a -

Take It Easy - 4 - 1

Verse 2:
Well, I'm a-standin' on a corner in Winslow, Arizona,
And such a fine sight to see:
It's a girl, my Lord, in a flatbed Ford
Slowin' down to take a look at me.

Chorus 2:
Come on, baby, don't say maybe.
I gotta know if your sweet love is gonna save me.
We may lose and we may win, though we will never be here again.
So open up, I'm climbin' in, so take it easy.
(To Guitar Solo:)

Verse 3:
Well, I'm a-runnin' down the road, tryin' to loosen my load,
Got a world of trouble on my mind.
Lookin' for a lover who won't blow my cover,
She's so hard to find.
(To Chorus:)

A HORSE WITH NO NAME

Words and Music by
DEWEY BUNNELL

A Horse with No Name - 3 - 1

Verse 2:
After two days in the desert sun
My skin began to turn red.
After three days in the desert fun
I was looking at a river bed.
And the story it told of a river that flowed
Made me sad to think it was dead.
You see, I've…
(To Chorus:)

Verse 3:
After nine days I let the horse run free
'Cause the desert had turned to sea.
There were plants and birds and rocks and things,
There were sand and hills and rings.
The ocean is a desert with its life underground
And the perfect disguise above.
Under the cities lies a heart made of ground,
But the humans will give no love.
You see, I've…
(To Chorus:)

BANJO CHORD DICTIONARY

A CHORDS

A	A	Amaj7	A6
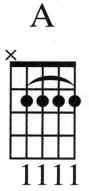	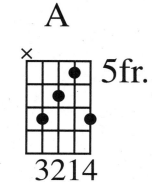 5fr.	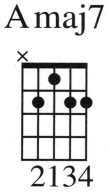	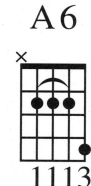
1111	3214	2134	1113

Am	Am	Am7	Am6
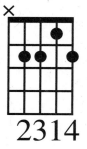	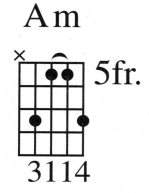 5fr.	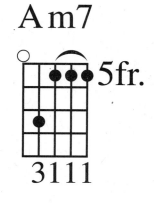 5fr.	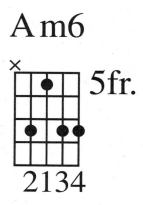 5fr.
2314	3114	3111	2134

A7	A7	A9	A13
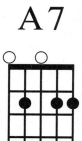	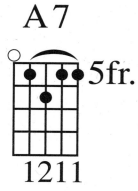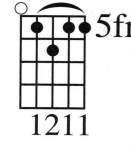 5fr.	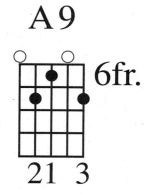 6fr.	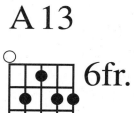 6fr.
2 34	1211	21 3	2134

Asus	A7sus	Adim7	A⁺
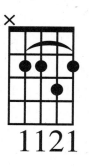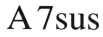	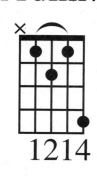	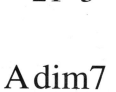	
1121	1121	1214	2113

B♭ (A♯) CHORDS*

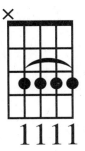

B♭

1111

B♭
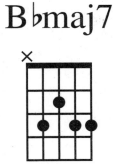
6fr.
3214

B♭maj7
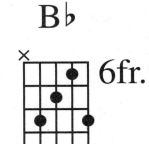
213

B♭6
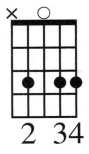
2 34

B♭m
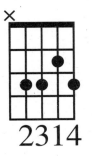
2314

B♭m
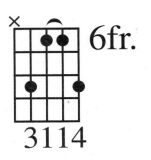
6fr.
3114

B♭m7
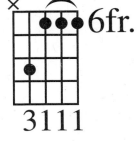
6fr.
3111

B♭m6
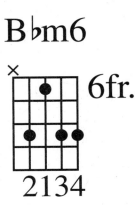
6fr.
2134

B♭7
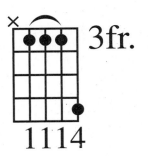
3fr.
1114

B♭7

6fr.
1211

B♭9
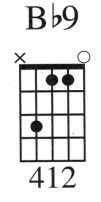
412

B♭13
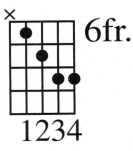
6fr.
1234

B♭sus
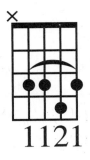
1121

B♭7sus
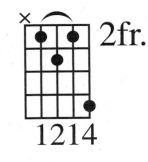
6fr.
1314

B♭dim7
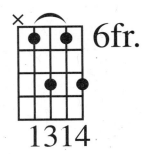
2fr.
1214

B♭+
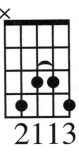
2113

*B♭ and A♯ are two names for the same note.

B CHORDS

B
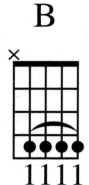
1111

B
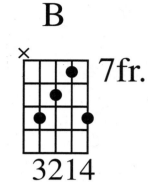
7fr.
3214

Bmaj7
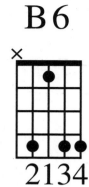
2134

B6
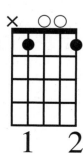
2134

Bm
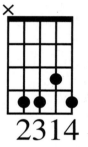
2314

Bm
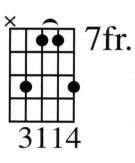
7fr.
3114

Bm7
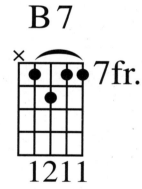
3124

Bm6
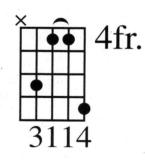
6fr.
1224

B7
2134

B7
7fr.
1211

B9
4231

B13
4fr.
3114

Bsus
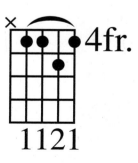
4fr.
1121

B7sus
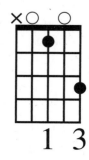
2fr.
3142

Bdim7
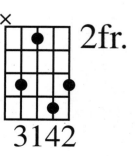
1 3

B+
1 2

45

C CHORDS

C

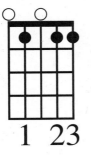
2 13

C
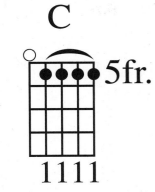
5fr.
1111

Cmaj7
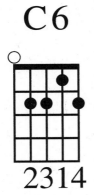
4fr.
2134

C6
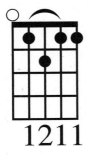
2314

Cm

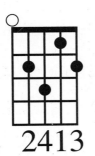
1 23

Cm
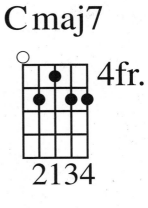
4fr.
2314

Cm7
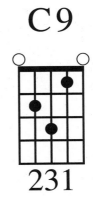
1311

Cm6
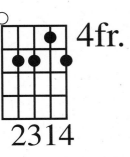
1211

C7

2413

C7
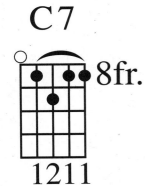
8fr.
1211

C9

231

C13
5fr.
3114

Csus
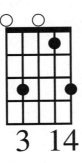
3 14

C7sus
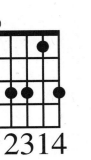
2314

Cdim7
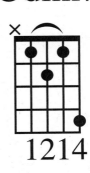
1214

C+
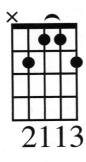
2113

C# (D♭) CHORDS*

C#
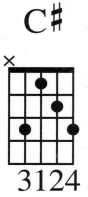
×
3124

C#
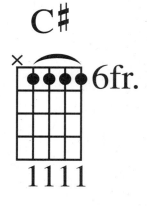
6fr.
1111

C#maj7
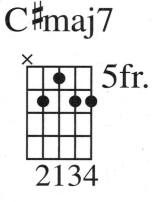
5fr.
2134

C#6
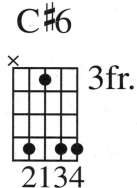
3fr.
2134

C#m

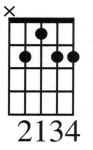
×
2134

C#m

5fr.
2314

C#m7
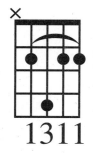
×
1311

C#m6
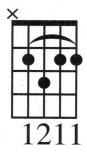
×
1211

C#7
×
2314

C#7
9fr.
1211

C#9
×
3421

C#13
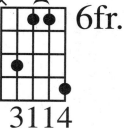
6fr.
3114

C#sus
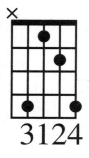
×
3124

C#7sus

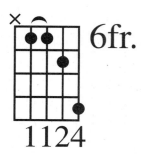
6fr.
1124

C#dim7
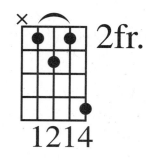
2fr.
1214

C#+
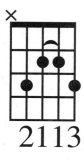
×
2113

*C# and D♭ are two names for the same note.

D CHORDS

D

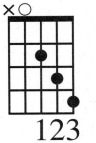

123

D

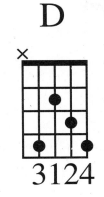

3124

Dmaj7

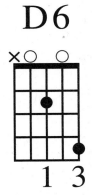

113

D6

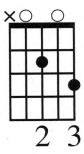

1 3

Dm

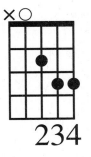

234

Dm

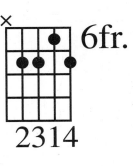 6fr.

2314

Dm7

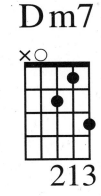

213

Dm6

2 3

D7

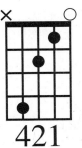

421

D7

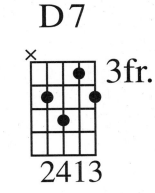 3fr.

2413

D9

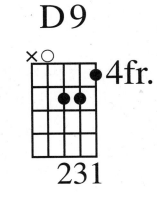 4fr.

231

D13

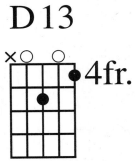 4fr.

2 1

Dsus

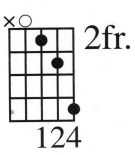 2fr.

124

D7sus

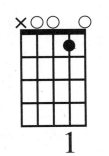

1

Ddim7

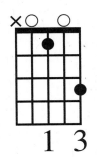

1 3

D+

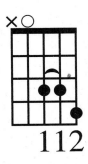

112

E♭ (D♯) CHORDS*

E♭
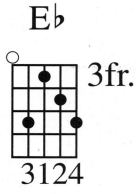
3fr.
3124

E♭
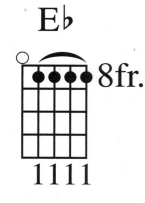
8fr.
1111

E♭maj7
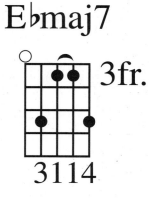
3fr.
3114

E♭6
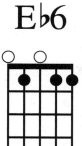
1 23

E♭m
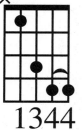

1344

E♭m
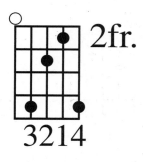
7fr.
2314

E♭m7
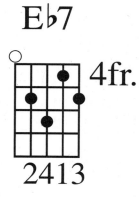
1324

E♭m6
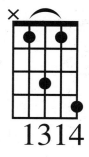
1314

E♭7

2fr.
3214

E♭7
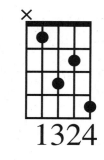
4fr.
2413

E♭9

1 23

E♭13
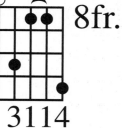
8fr.
3114

E♭sus
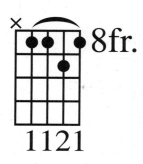
8fr.
1121

E♭7sus

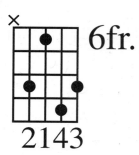
6fr.
2143

E♭dim7
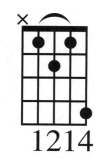
1214

E♭+
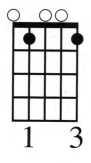
1 3

*E♭ and D♯ are two names for the same note.

E CHORDS

E
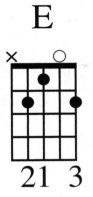
21 3

E
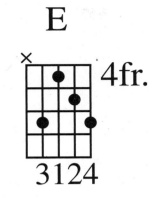
4fr.
3124

Emaj7
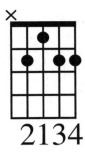
31 2

E6

2134

Em
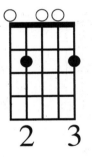

2 3

Em
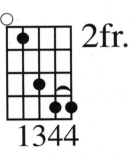
2fr.
1344

Em7
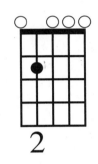
2

Em6
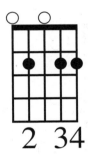
2 34

E7
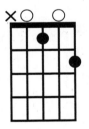
E7
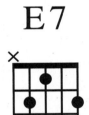
2143

E9
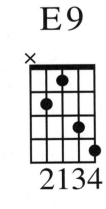
2134

E13
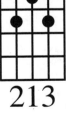
213

Esus
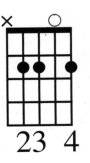
23 4

E7sus
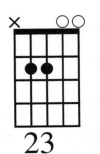
23

Edim7
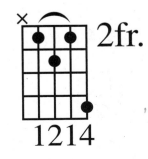
2fr.
1214

E+
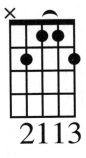
2113

F CHORDS

F
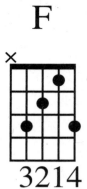
3214

F
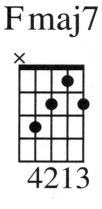
5fr.
3124

Fmaj7
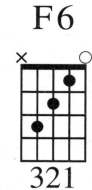
4213

F6

321

Fm
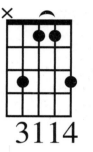
3114

Fm
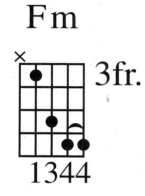
3fr.
1344

Fm7
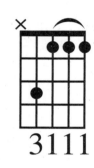
3111

Fm6
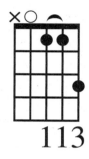
113

F7
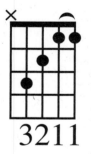
3211

F7
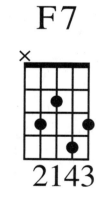
2143

F9

3211

F13

3241

Fsus
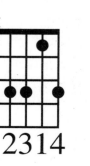
2314

F7sus
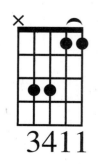
3411

Fdim7
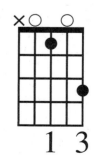
1   3

F+
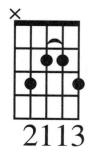
2113

F♯ (G♭) CHORDS*

F♯
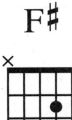
3214

F♯
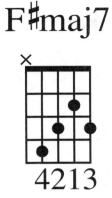
6fr.
3124

F♯maj7
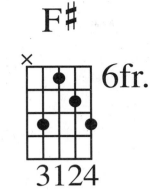
4213

F♯6

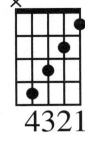
4321

F♯m
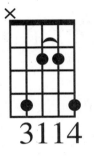
3114

F♯m
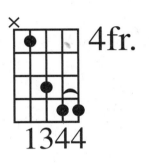
4fr.
1344

F♯m7

3111

F♯m6
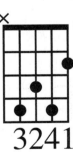
1234

F♯7
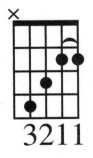

3211

F♯7
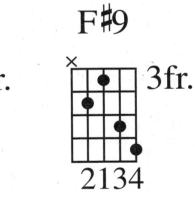
3fr.
2143

F♯9
3fr.
2134

F♯13
3241

F♯sus
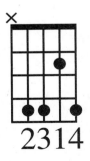
2314

F♯7sus
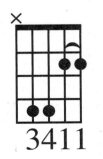
3411

F♯dim7
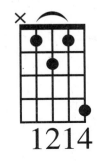
1214

F♯+
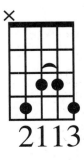
2113

*F♯ and G♭ are two names for the same note.

G CHORDS

G

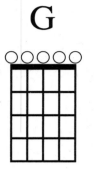

G

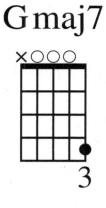
3fr.
3214

Gmaj7

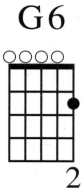
3

G6

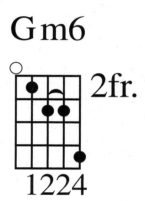
2

Gm

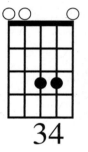
34

Gm

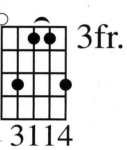
3fr.
3114

Gm7

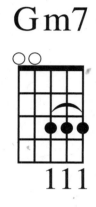
111

Gm6

2fr.
1224

G7

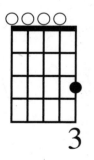
3

G7

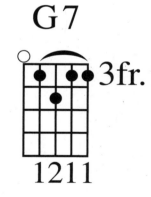
3fr.
1211

G9

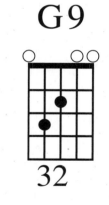
32

G13

3fr.
3241

Gsus

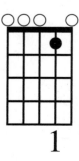
1

G7sus

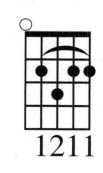
13

Gdim7

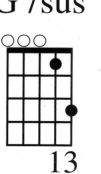
1211

G+

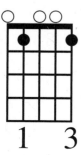
1   3

A♭ (G♯) CHORDS*

A♭
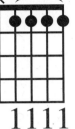
1111

A♭
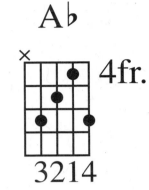
3214

A♭maj7
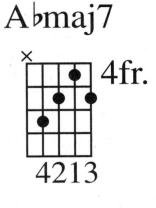
4213

A♭6
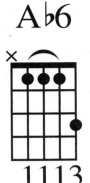
1113

A♭m
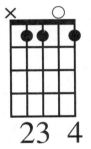
23 4

A♭m
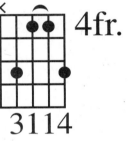
3114

A♭m7
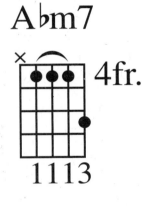
1113

A♭m6
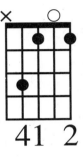
41 2

A♭7

1114

A♭7
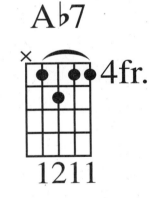
1211

A♭9
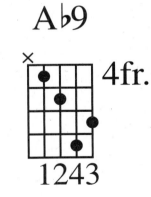
1243

A♭13
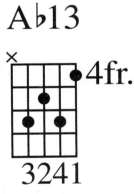
3241

A♭sus
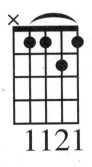
1121

A♭7sus
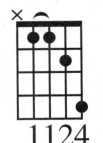
1124

A♭dim7
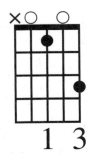
1 3

A♭+
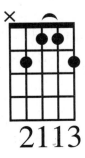
2113

*A♭ and G♯ are two names for the same note.

THE BEST OF
CLASSIC ROCK
GUITAR TAB!

Hotel California
Eagles
(00-24550) Authentic
Guitar TAB, $19.95

**The Very Best
of Eagles**
Eagles
(00-PGM0404) Authentic
Guitar TAB, $34.95

Workingman's Dead
Grateful Dead
(00-PGM0513) Authentic
Guitar TAB, $22.95

Greatest Hits
James Taylor
(00-GF0623) Authentic
Guitar TAB, $22.95

Songbook
John Denver
(00-PGM0113) Authentic
Guitar TAB, $21.95

**Guitar Anthology
Series**
Journey
(00-0511B) Authentic
Guitar TAB, $24.95

**Led Zeppelin I–V
(Boxed Set)**
Led Zeppelin
(00-PG9635A) Authentic
Guitar TAB, $99.95

Mothership
Led Zeppelin
(00-30373) Authentic
Guitar TAB, $34.95

Greatest Hits
Mötley Crüe
(00-PGM0309) Authentic
Guitar TAB, $24.95

Cowboys from Hell
Pantera
(00-25955) Authentic
Guitar TAB, $24.95

Guitar TAB Anthology
Pink Floyd
(52-ML1909) Authentic
Guitar TAB, $22.95

The Wall
Pink Floyd
(52-ML2122) Authentic
Guitar TAB, $22.95

**Singles Collection:
The London Years**
Rolling Stones
(00-P0870GTX)
Guitar/TAB/Vocal, $29.95

**Guitar Anthology
Series**
Rush
(00-PG9530) Authentic
Guitar TAB, $24.95

Ultimate Santana
Carlos Santana
(00-29046) Authentic
Guitar TAB, $24.95

**The Best of
Both Worlds**
Van Halen
(00-PGM0418) Authentic
Guitar TAB, $29.95

Guitar Songbook
Van Morrison
(00-29972) Authentic
Guitar TAB, $21.95

**Songs You Know by
Heart: Jimmy Buffett's
Greatest Hits**
Jimmy Buffett
(00-P0723GTX) Authentic
Guitar TAB, $18.95

AVAILABLE at YOUR FAVORITE MUSIC RETAILER

Alfred Music Publishing
LEARN · TEACH · PLAY